Circular Scroll Saw Designs

Circular Scroll Saw Designs

Fretwork Patterns for Trivets, Coasters, Wall Art & More

CHARLES R. HAND

Fox Chapel
PUBLISHING

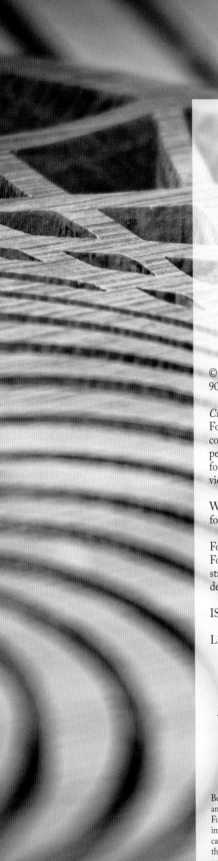

Dedication

For all the times I interrupt your day to say, "Debbie, do you have a minute? Come see what I am working on." You are my biggest fan, and without your constant support and encouragement, this book would not have been possible. Thank you for giving me that nudge I needed to do this. I love you, Deborah Jean, with all of my heart. This is your book as much as mine.

Wood grain images for select projects courtesy of Shutterstock.com and the following creators: Leszek Maziarz, yoshi0511, wk1003mike, Guiyuan Chen

For a printable PDF of the patterns used in this book, please contact Fox Chapel Publishing at customerservice@foxchapelpublishing.com, stating the ISBN and title of the book in the subject line, along with details of the pattern(s) you require.

ISBN 978-1-4971-0150-0

Library of Congress Control Number: 2020948704

To learn more about the other great books from Fox Chapel Publishing, or to find a retailer near you, call toll-free 800-457-9112 or visit us at *www.FoxChapelPublishing.com.*

We are always looking for talented authors. To submit an idea, please send a brief inquiry to acquisitions@foxchapelpublishing.com.

Printed in Singapore
First printing

Introduction

My journey with and love for the scroll saw began in 2005 when I was looking for something to do during those long winter months in Canada. I discovered I could combine my love for graphic design and photography in wood via a scroll saw. I learned everything then, from fretwork to intarsia to segmentation. Before long, I was making gifts for my entire family and designing my own patterns. Ever since, I've been continually inspired by the endless possibilities waiting at the tip of my saw blade.

I'm excited to share that passion with you here, in *Circular Scroll Saw Designs*. In this book, I share everything you need to know to get started with fretwork, along with 27 of my favorite scroll saw patterns suited to a wide range of skill levels. I cover essential materials, provide a tool guide, and walk you through basic techniques—with great tips and tricks I've gathered over the last fifteen-plus years. I also include information on finishing for a beautiful end result.

I've sized most of the designs provided to 8" (20.3cm), which is perfect for a trivet, but you can enlarge or shrink these patterns to create so much more. You can cut coasters, wall art, plaques, serving trays—just about anything! What better gift to give your loved ones or friends on special occasions than something that is both beautiful and functional?

All it takes to create these projects is a good piece of wood, some sharp blades, a steady hand, and a little bit of patience. Follow the lines and you will be pleasantly surprised with the end results. Scroll sawing is a very rewarding and fun hobby for me, and I know that it will be (or already is) for you as well.

I hope you enjoy cutting these patterns as much as I enjoyed designing them.

Charles R. Hand

Charles R. Hand
St. Catharines, Ontario, Canada

Contents

Part 1: Getting Started 8

  Materials and Tools 10

  Basic Techniques 17

  Finishing. 23

Part 2: Gallery of Projects and Ideas . . .26

Part 3: Step-by-Step Projects 38

  Project 1: Teddy Bear Trivet 40

  Project 2: Spring Flower Lazy Susan 48

  Project 3: Summer Love Plaque 54

40

48

68

70

76

78

80

82

88

90

92

94

100

102

104

106

54

62

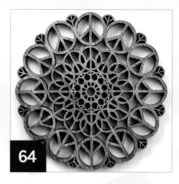

64

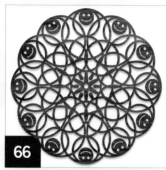

66

72

74

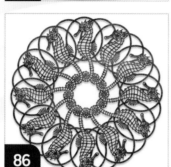

84

86

96

98

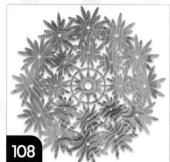

108

Part 4: Patterns 60

Starflake Trivet 62

Peace Trivet 64

Happy Day Trivet 66

Easter Bunny Trivet 68

Shamrock Trivet 70

Delicate Spiral Trivet 72

Snowflake Trivet 74

Angelfish Bowl Trivet/Plaque 76

Hummingbird Trivet/Plaque 78

Butterfly Plaque 80

Ornate Flower Trivet 82

Sunburst Trivet/Plaque 84

Seahorse Trivet 86

Guitar Trivet 88

Mandala Trivet 90

Fancy Circle Trivet 92

Square Spiral Trivet 94

Christmas Tree Trivet 96

Heart Coaster 98

Peace Coaster 100

Anchor Coaster 102

Elaborate Plaque 104

Dragonfly Plaque 106

Spring Flower Plaque 108

About the Author 110

Acknowledgments 110

Praise for Charles Hand 111

Index 112

PART 1

Getting Started

Are you ready to learn everything you need to know about the materials and tools, basic process, and finishing options for creating any and all of the trivets, coasters, and plaques featured in this book? If you're an experienced scroll sawyer, you may know some of this information already, but it's a good idea to review it regardless so that you understand the approach for the projects in the book and can make the best choices for your work—whether it's about what wood to use for a coaster versus a trivet, what kind of sanding tools are best for which tasks, or what finish to use if you want to hang your work outdoors. It's all in the following pages!

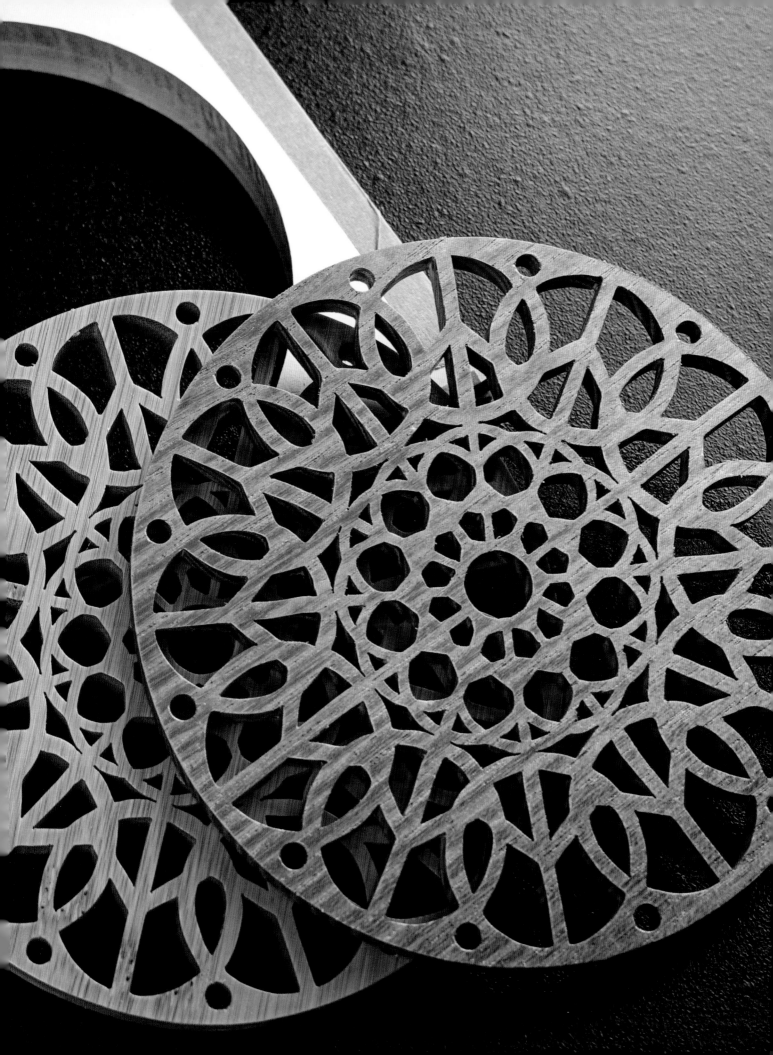

Materials and Tools

Wood Selection

Most types of wood will work just fine for trivets, coasters, and plaques. Oak, walnut, teak, maple, cherry, and poplar (all hardwoods), as well as cedar and pine (both softwoods), are popular choices. I prefer wood with a nice grain pattern, so I tend to cut a lot of oak. Bamboo, which is a grass rather than a tree wood, is also a great alternative and less expensive than most hardwoods. Over the last few years, it has come to be a very popular choice and substitute for hardwood floors and building materials. For some of the projects in this book, I repurposed a few bamboo cutting boards purchased from the kitchen section of a big-box store.

Some hardwoods, as well as bamboo, are available at stores such as Lowe's and Home Depot in the U.S. and Canada, but only in limited varieties. Local family-run lumber mills or exotic wood stores are good sources for hardwoods, as they often carry more options.

Baltic birch plywood is another specific product I recommend for many of the projects in this book. It cuts well and does not chip like big-box-store plywood does. The keyword to search for when shopping for it is "Baltic"; Russian or Finnish are the most popular varieties. It normally comes in full 5' (1.5m) square sheets in various thicknesses; for some of the projects in this book, I recommend ¼" (6mm), ⅜" (10mm), ½" (13mm), ⅝" (16mm), and ¾" (19mm) thicknesses. Most of these thicknesses are available at specialty lumber stores, but not at big-box stores. Many cabinet makers use Baltic birch plywood, though, so you may be able to get some from one near you. You can also get some thicknesses in smaller sheet sizes at select big-box craft stores.

To some degree, the kind of wood you select will depend on the item you are making—read on.

TRIVETS FOR STOVE-ADJACENT USE

If you are making a trivet that will be exposed to very hot temperatures, use a hardwood or bamboo to withstand the heat of a boiling pot or a casserole dish straight out of the oven. (Of course, wood will burn if you get it too close to a lit stove, so use caution.) I use oak for this application mostly because of the availability where I live, but if you live in a different region, you may find that a different hardwood is more widely available to you. Make sure the trivet is at least ½" (13mm) to 1" (25mm) thick; any

The thickness of your wood will largely depend on the particular use you want to make of the item.

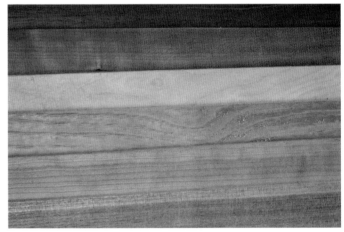

A particular piece of wood's coloring and grain will have a major effect on the look of your finished piece.

You can cut up bamboo cutting boards to make spectacular scroll-sawn projects.

thinner than that and the extreme heat might still transfer to the surface you're trying to protect. Plus, the piece will simply be flimsy and more likely to break.

TABLE TRIVETS AND PLAQUES

Any of the wood types listed will work fine for trivets that will be used for warm or hot dishes being set on a table for serving, as well as for decorative plaques. Baltic birch plywood is a favorite for many scrollers; I have cut many items using it. A good thickness for a table trivet or plaque is ¼" (6mm) to ½" (13mm).

COASTERS

A good thickness for coasters is ¼" (6mm) to ⅜" (10mm), to keep them somewhat low-profile. Many big-box stores carry ¼" (6mm)– to ⅜" (10mm)–thick hardwoods and softwoods, such as poplar, cedar, oak, maple, and bamboo. Exotic wood stores and family-operated lumber mills often carry many more wood varieties that you can use to make coasters.

What Are You Making? Trivets, Coasters, and Plaques

Before we get started, it's important that you understand the basic terms that will be used for the projects and designs throughout this book.

Trivet: A trivet, often made from various materials such as wood, ceramic, and metal, is used as a sacrificial piece to protect tabletop surfaces from hot casserole dishes, bowls, pots, and the like. There are many alternative names for a trivet, such as rest, stand, support, tripod, pedestal, and platform, to name a few.

Coaster: Coasters can be made from many of the same materials as trivets, including paper. Paper versions are sometimes called beermats, and they are used to help absorb liquid into the mat or coaster. Because we are using wood, the coasters in this book only serve to help protect surfaces from hot and cold beverages, not to soak up moisture the way a paper coaster might.

Plaque: Often made of wood or metal, a plaque normally serves as a decorative wall piece or a centerpiece on a dining room table, kitchen table, or buffet cabinet. A plaque can be painted, stained, or simply left as is to showcase the raw wood.

Trivets, coasters, and wall plaques are the three main kinds of items you can make using the patterns in this book.

Tools

There are several tools you'll need to complete the projects in this book and create clean, durable, useful items. If you are a beginner scroller who is unfamiliar with any of the tools listed here, more detail about each one follows, including my personal recommendations for sizes and brands (where applicable). Each tool can be purchased at your local home improvement store. Not all these tools are essential for creating the projects (see the individual descriptions to learn which ones you can do without), but the nonessential tools will make your life easier, so if you have the money to invest, I recommend acquiring them all.

- Scroll saw
- Table saw, radial arm saw, or sliding compound saw
- Bench sander
- Palm sander
- Electric hand drill or drill press
- Drill bits (³⁄₆₄" [1.2mm] and ¹⁄₁₆" [1.6mm] or #56 [1.2mm] and #52 [1.6mm], and larger)
- Various blades: #3–#5 skip-tooth and/or reverse tooth (manufacturers of choice); #3–#5 Modified Geometry is a Pégas brand that I recommend.

- Assorted needle files (optional)
- Compressed air (optional)
- Painter's pyramids (optional)
- Scissors
- Assorted paintbrushes
- Soft cloth
- Tack cloth

This is my personal collection of most of the tools and supplies I use to prepare, cut, and finish my fretwork projects (excluding the larger machines like the scroll saw and drill press): plastic bin for oil (1); oil and various varnishes (2); spray glue (3); acrylic paint (4); various scroll saw blades (5); palm sander (6); painter's pyramid cones (7); mask (8); sandpaper in assorted grits (9); removable contact paper (10); painter's tape (11); scissors (12); shop towels (13); plastic gloves (14); various drill bits (15); tack cloth (16); various paintbrushes (17); stick-on protector (felt) pads (18); needle files (19).

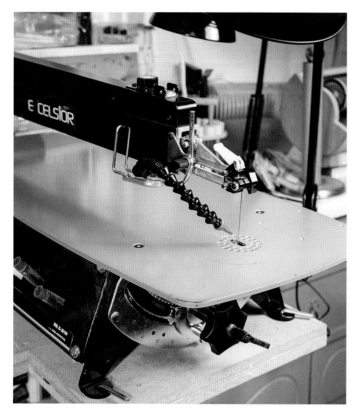

Scroll saw: Use a small bench-mounted or stand-mounted scroll saw to cut the detailed, intricate wood designs that this book focuses on. Saws come in a range of sizes and prices, from beginner/intermediate saws to professional saws. Sizes 16" (40cm) to 21" (53cm) are the most popular.

Bench sander: A large electric, stationary sander is useful for shaping and smoothing wood in conjunction with a palm sander. Instead of moving the sanding tool over the wood, you move the wood against the sanding tool. I like to use a bench sander after cutting a piece to be used on a trivet. I find that when using a larger sander like this, I can smooth the edges and surfaces quicker than with a palm sander. The bench sander pictured is a 2-in-1 belt and disc sander.

Table saw, radial arm saw (pictured), or sliding compound saw: A large stand or bench-mounted saw like any of the examples listed will make cutting square wood shapes quicker, easier, and more precise than simply sawing by hand. (But you can, of course, cut your blanks by hand if you don't have any of these tools.)

Palm sander: This small handheld electric detail sander is great for smoothing wood surfaces before scrolling. It will save you time and elbow grease when compared to sandpaper (but sandpaper is a viable alternative if you don't have a palm sander).

Electric hand drill or drill press (pictured): Use a handheld or stationary drill to drill all the necessary pilot holes in your wood before you start scrolling.

Drill bits (³⁄₆₄" [1.2mm] and ¹⁄₁₆" [1.6mm] or #56 [1.2mm] and #52 [1.6mm], and larger): Choose drill bits relative to the size of each fretwork pilot hole. In general, you will want to use smaller drill bits for very small frets. I recommend sizes for every project in this book. There are also some circular design features, like eyes and flower centers, that will be easier to simply drill to size rather than scroll.

Various blades: See more detail about blades and blade selection on page 18.

Assorted needle files (optional): These small handheld files are great for removing fuzzies and burrs from the wood surface in between cuts. They make it easy to get into tight angles and curves.

Compressed air (optional): Use a handheld compressed air canister or larger stationary electrical air compressor to remove dust particles between cutouts and from the surface of the wood.

Painter's pyramids (optional): These small, plastic pyramid shapes allow you to neatly support wood while it is drying after applications of spray varnish, paint, or oil.

Scissors: You'll need a simple pair of scissors to cut out your patterns and contact paper.

Assorted paintbrushes: If you want to apply oil finishes or paint your pieces, you'll need paintbrushes in suitable sizes.

Soft cloth: If you want to apply oil finishes, you'll need a soft cloth for removing and buffing the oil.

Tack cloth: Always have some tack cloths on hand to quickly clean off dust from your work and your work surfaces.

Supplies

Most of the supplies you'll need to complete the projects in this book are ones you probably already have lying around in your workshop or home, like painter's tape and sandpaper. You might need to run to your local craft store to find a few of them, like spray adhesive and contact paper. Make sure you have the following essential items before beginning a project, as well as any of the optional items you may need in order to finish a project in a particular way (more on finishing on page 23).

- Wood of choice
- Contact paper (such as removable Con-Tact® Brand Creative Covering™ or similar) (for applying patterns to wood)
- Spray adhesive or all-purpose glue stick (for applying paper patterns to contact paper)
- Blue painter's tape or Frog® tape (for taping edge/perimeter of wood if stack cutting)

- 180- to 220-grit sandpaper
- Danish oil or mineral oil (optional but recommended)
- Wood sealer (optional) (when not using Danish or mineral oil)
- Craft paints (optional)
- Clear lacquer (spray or brush-on), heat and exterior grade (optional)
- Paper towels

Use contact paper to apply paper patterns to wood so that they are secure while scrolling but a cinch to remove with no residue.

Stack cutting is a great way to cut multiples of items like coasters at once; use painter's tape to easily and temporarily attach the pieces of wood before cutting.

If you want to go for a stylized, vivid—even festive—effect, acrylic paints are a cheap and easy way to jazz up a finished piece.

Danish oil is a great finishing product that protects the wood and adds a smooth, satin finish.

Top Tip for Scroll Saw Care

I take special care of my scroll saws. My oldest saw is a 1998 Excalibur 30" (76cm) made in Canada, and this old saw, as with my others, is in pristine condition only because I treat it well. After cutting approximately twenty cutouts, I thoroughly vacuum the underside and table, freeing it from dust. At the end of the day, I treat my saw to a WD-40® bath. This is not actually a bath, of course, but I spray a thin coat of WD-40 over the tabletop and onto a dry cloth, then wipe down the entire table, blade clamp, and arm. I do this after every use.

I have always protected my tools with WD-40 and cannot recommend this product more heartily. There is no silicone in WD-40, so it will not cause any harm to your tools. Many woodworkers use paste wax to protect the tables of their saws, which seems to work well too, but my preference is WD-40. In fact, I often close up my shop from May through September, and the protection offered by the WD-40 cleanup I do before closing up always lasts until I open up again for more scroll sawing in the fall—there is never any rust.

Treat your saws and equipment well, and they will last for a very long time.

1 Vacuum not just the table but also the underside of your saw after approximately every twenty cutouts while working.

2 For end-of-day cleanup, start by spraying a thin coat of WD-40 directly onto the saw tabletop.

3 Wipe down the entire table, making sure your cloth has enough product on it. Spray more product directly on the cloth if needed.

4 Don't forget to also wipe down the blade clamp and arm.

Basic Techniques

Basic Process

Any project should follow the same essential basic process described here. There are three phases: preparing the blank with the pattern (Preparation), doing the actual pattern cutting (Cutting), and cleaning up the completed piece (Wrap-Up). For more photos, detail, and guidance about the process, see the step-by-step projects starting on page 38.

Preparation

1. Cut your blank a minimum of ½" (1.3cm) larger than the pattern you are cutting. For example, for a circular trivet that is 8" (20.3cm) in diameter, cut the square blank to a minimum of 8½" (21.6cm).
2. Thoroughly sand each side and edge of the blank with a palm or bench sander.
3. Remove all dust with compressed air and/or a tack cloth.
4. Cut a piece of removable contact paper. Remove the thin protective backing and attach the paper to the top of the blank. Make sure there are no air bubbles, repositioning as needed.
5. Apply spray adhesive to the back side of the paper pattern. Allow the glue to set for approximately one minute or until tacky, then attach the back side of the pattern to the contact paper. Remove all air bubbles by applying pressure with your thumb and pushing the bubbles outward to the exterior edge of the pattern paper.

Cutting

6. Drill all pilot holes for the blade throughout the entire pattern. Also drill any specific feature holes (fret holes that only need to be drilled, not scrolled).
7. Position your blank in your saw, being sure you are following all safety measures and manufacturer's instructions for your particular saw. In general, you will first loosen the top or bottom of the blade from the chuck head, then thread it through the drilled blade-entry hole. Tighten the blade in both chuck heads and tension the blade (see more about blade tension on page 20).
8. Cut one entire fret at a time. Start cutting frets from the middle of the pattern, working your way outward. Follow any specific instructions and guidance given for your chosen pattern.
9. Cut the exterior outline last.

Wrap-Up

10. Once you have made all cuts, peel off the removable contact paper and pattern.
11. Sand the front and back surfaces again, including the perimeter edge.
12. If necessary, use needle files to sand hard-to-reach places.
13. Remove sanding dust with compressed air or a tack cloth.

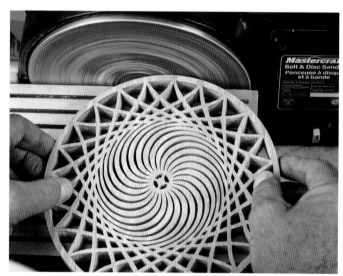

Sanding with a belt and disc sander

Using a needle file to get into hard-to-reach places

Blade Selection

Selecting blades for your project depends very much on the wood type and thickness that you are using. Thicker, denser woods tend to require larger blades; a ½" (13mm) slab of wenge (a very hard wood) will require a larger, tougher blade than the same thickness of pine (a softer wood). For blade sizes, smaller numbers indicate smaller blades; a #1 blade is tiny and a #9 blade is large. The most popular blade sizes for projects like the ones in this book are #3, #5, and #7 blades. I often cut up to 1" (25mm)–thick wood using a #5 blade; it is my blade of choice when cutting trivets, plaques, and coasters. I recommend that you try various blade sizes and types to see what works best for you.

To make the projects in this book, I recommend either skip-tooth blades or reverse tooth blades. **Skip-tooth blades (A)** are a good choice for cutting thicker wood. Every other tooth is removed, therefore creating less friction and reducing burning of the wood when cutting. **Reverse tooth blades (B)** have a small section at the bottom of the blade where the teeth are facing up instead of down. This means that they cut not only in a downward motion but also in an upward motion, leaving a cleaner, smoother finish, which means less sanding for you.

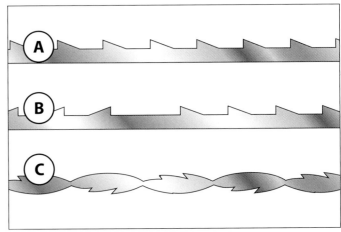

Simplified profiles of skip-tooth (A), reverse tooth (B), and spiral (C) blades

You can find these kinds of blades produced by popular brands such as Olsen, Niqua, Flying Dutchman, Pégas, and Delta, to name a few. These blades will have a kerf on one side, so they will wander left or right when cutting; plan your cuts accordingly and do not fight the pull to left or right. Work with it. I personally like the Modified Geometry blades made by Pégas (Switzerland), as there is no kerf to pull left or right, therefore allowing the blade to cut perfectly straight. Modified Geometry blades cut more aggressively, though, so it may take time for you to get accustomed to them.

For most of the patterns in this book, I do not recommend spiral-tooth blades, as they will not leave a clean finish. **Spiral-tooth blades (C),** with their teeth on all sides, are great to use for wavy lines, such as in the Butterfly Plaque (page 80), but not for straight lines. I do a lot of portrait cutting and use spiral-tooth blades for that application, but I rarely use them for trivets, plaques, or coasters when even cuts matter for aesthetics and a quality finish.

There are several other types of blades for scroll saws that have different features and applications; examples include standard tooth blades, double tooth cut blades, two-way cut blades, crown-tooth blades, and more. Because I do not recommend the use of any of these blades for the projects in this book, I won't cover them in detail here, but if you prefer using any particular blades, feel free to see if you like their result when creating your trivets, coasters, and plaques.

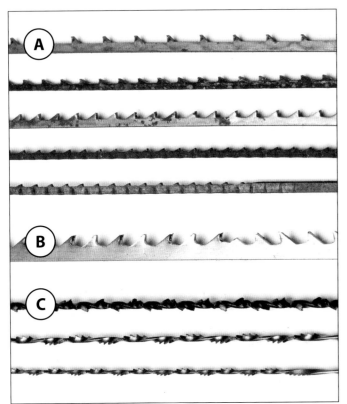

Examples of skip-tooth (A), reverse tooth (B), and spiral (C) blades

Cutting

GENERAL SAFETY

When operating power equipment, always think about safety—otherwise you may find yourself in a hospital emergency room. Fully read the safety section of the manuals that came with your equipment before operating it.

Although scroll saws are one of the safest large tools to operate, accidents can happen if you are not paying attention. Keep your fingers in front of your work and not on top, where the blade clamp can hit your fingers. There is enough force in that clamp when in motion to do some serious damage to your knuckles. I tend to hold my work from the sides, feeding it into the blade, but never where my fingers are under that fast-moving blade clamp head. Keep your fingers clear as well when operating bench sanders and power saws.

While working, wear comfortable clothing that is not loose enough to potentially get caught in a tool like a table saw. Also, wear safety glasses if possible to protect your eyes from flying debris.

I cannot stress enough the importance of wearing a good quality dust mask or respirator—always wear one. Dust particles from many woods may be harmful to your health or irritate your lungs.

Because scroll saws produce fine dust that can float in the air for several minutes, it is a good idea to ventilate the room that you are in. I have a ceiling air filtration unit in my shop and also one that I made from an old furnace fan. If you don't have the room to install one of these, you can use a tabletop unit. A box fan with a filter installed to one side works well and is less costly than a ceiling-mounted unit. If you have a window in your shop,

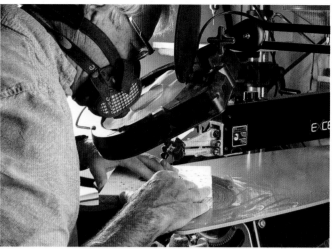

Wear a dust mask and glasses or goggles; I'm not wearing goggles here because the large magnifying glass is protecting my eyes.

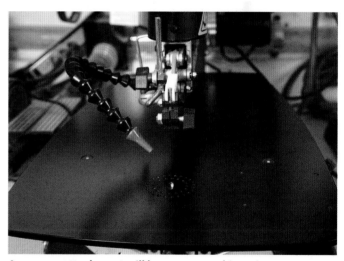

A vacuum attachment will keep your working piece consistently clear of debris.

Tip

Fogging up of glasses is often an issue when you wear glasses and a dust mask at the same time. I have tried many masks over the years and found a favorite that doesn't fog up my glasses: the GVS Elipse P100 Respirator. I love the snug fit and low profile. Here is a list of other masks you can consider, all made by the 3M™ company, that are also very popular for woodworkers: Rugged Comfort Quick Latch Half Facepiece Respirator, Half Facepiece Respirator, Cool Flow™ Sanding and Fiberglass Respirator, and Professional Multi-Purpose Respirator with Drop-Down. There are many companies who make quality dust masks and respirators, so do your research.

Kerf-test squaring

Squaring with a square

installing a fan to draw the air out works well. If your shop is in your house instead of a garage or workshop, cover the intake of your house's air system in that room to prevent dusty air from entering the air-handling system and dispersing throughout the house.

A vacuum attachment on your scroll saw can help keep the air somewhat clearer and your work cleaner, but it is not a replacement for a dust mask and good ventilation.

SQUARING UP YOUR TABLE

Most scroll saws have an adjustable table that allows you to make cuts at different angles. There are times when you want the saw set at an angle, but most cutting is done with the blade perpendicular to the table. If the table is even slightly off-square, the cuts will be angled. This may not be a big deal in coasters and trivets, but it will definitely interfere with puzzle pieces, intarsia, segmentation, and many other types of scrolling projects, so it's good to train yourself in best practices.

The most common method for squaring a table uses a small metal square, or right angle tool. Set the square flat on the saw table against a blade that has been inserted and tensioned. Adjust the table to form a 90-degree angle to the blade.

The cutting-through method is also popular. Saw through a piece of scrap wood at least ¾" (19mm) thick and check the angle of the cut using a square. Adjust the table until you get a perfectly square cut.

You can also use the kerf-test method. Take a 1¾" (45mm)-thick piece of scrap wood and cut about ¹⁄₁₆" (2mm) into it. Stop the saw, back the blade out, and spin the wood around to the back of the blade. If the blade slips easily into the kerf, the table is square. If it doesn't, adjust the table and perform the test again until the blade slips in easily.

BLADE TENSION

Before inserting a blade, completely remove the tension. Clamp both ends of the blade into the blade holders and adjust the tension. Push on the blade with your finger. It should flex no more than ⅛" (3mm) forward, backward, or side to side. A blade that does not have enough tension will wander. It will also flex from side to side, making for irregular or angled cuts. If you press too hard on a loose blade, it will usually snap. A blade that has too much tension is more susceptible to breaking and tends to pull out of the blade holders. In general, it is better to make the blade too tight than too loose.

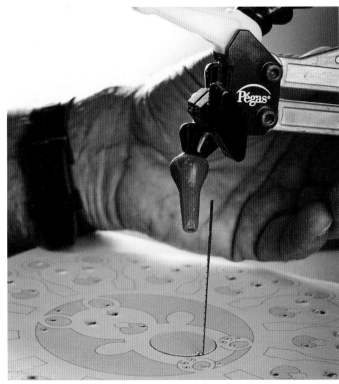

Always check your blade tension any time you have to remove and reinsert a blade.

Tip

I use a lighted magnifying glass for more accurate cuts. When looking through the glass, I find that the accuracy of my cuts improves. Try it!

CUTTING SAFELY

I can't overemphasize the importance of changing blades often. As soon as a blade starts to slow, burn the wood, loosen in the blade clamp, or wander, it is time to toss it out and bring in a new one. Blades are cheap and wood is not. Make sure you have enough blades on hand to complete your project so that you are not tempted to push through to the end with a dying blade. If you do a lot of scrolling, buy blades by the gross to save on cost.

Do not rush your project, and never force the wood into the blade. Rushing and forcing will cause the blade to wander, dull more quickly, and create uneven lines, therefore ruining your project. Forcing can also cause premature wear on your expensive scroll saw. Take your time and do it right. Always allow your saw to do the work, and ease the wood into the blade.

You can choose what speed to run the saw; I recommend setting it at just under half speed. Many people cut full tilt without an issue, but my preference is to cut slowly, simply following the pattern lines as I go until the work is done. The result is clean and visually pleasing. There is nothing worse than spending hours cutting a piece only to have a cutout get away from you due to a wandering and dull blade.

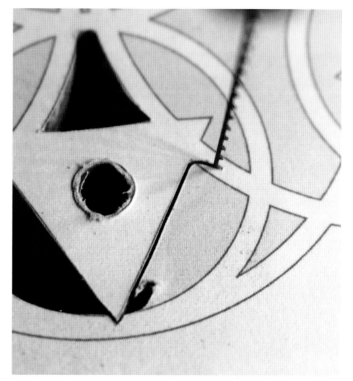

Even I sometimes make mistakes! Just take your time and do not rush—slow and steady makes the cut clean and accurate.

STACK CUTTING

Stack cutting lets you cut several pieces of a project—or multiple projects, like coasters—at one time. Essentially, you attach several blanks together and cut them as one unit. My favorite way to attach the blanks is with painter's tape, as shown here, but you can also do it with hot glue between the blanks or even nails. If you use nails, cut and sand them flush to avoid scratching your table.

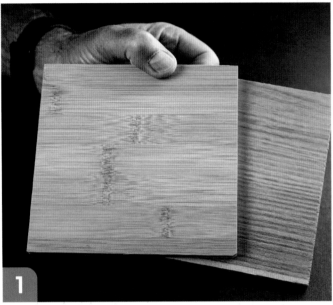

Prep your pieces of wood. Here, I've used bamboo (top) and sassafras.

Attach the pattern to one piece like normal, then stack the two pieces and securely tape them together using painter's tape. You can do up to three pieces at a time as long as the stack doesn't get too thick—stay at or below ¾" (19mm).

Scroll the stack just like normal.

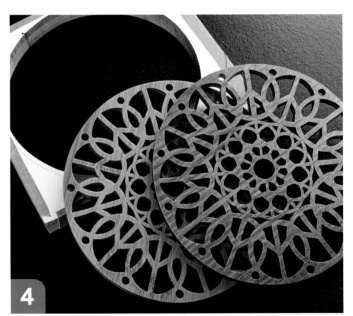

You get two coasters for the price of one!

Finishing

How you choose to finish (or not finish) each project is totally up to you. You will want to keep in mind the use of the item, however. For example, a trivet to be used habitually for hot casserole dishes is essentially a sacrificial piece between the countertop and the dish. In time and with extensive use, any trivet may discolor and, in some cases, show burn marks. That is to be expected.

Some woodworkers believe that a trivet meant for extended hot use is better not finished with any product at all. This can work, but I personally find that hand-rubbed mineral oil or Danish oil is a great choice for finishing such trivets. It protects the wood and creates a nice, smooth, satin finish that allows the grain of the wood to pop. The other nice thing about using an oil finish is that you can re-sand the piece and add a fresh new coat or two when it begins to show wear from use.

Follow these steps to finish with oil. You can also apply oil with a brush, instead of dipping; the general instructions still apply.

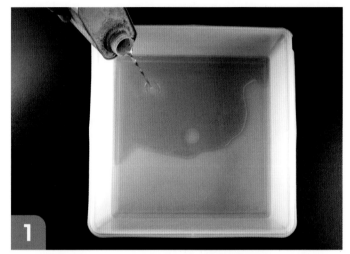

1 Pour a layer of oil into a large pan; plastic storage containers are excellent to use for this process. Put on gloves.

2 Dip your piece into the oil-filled pan. The oil will spread well and get into those hard-to-reach corners and cutouts that a medium like acrylic paint will not. Allow it to settle into the wood for anywhere from two to ten minutes.

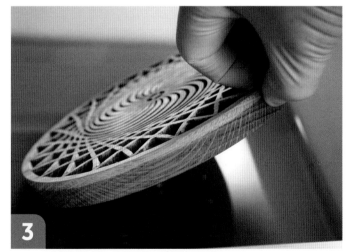

3 If your oil bath isn't deep enough to completely submerge the piece, remove it and dip the other side to ensure full coverage. Allow the oil to settle again, then remove the piece from the bath.

4 Use a soft cloth or towel to rub off the excess oil. Set the piece on painter's pyramids and allow it to dry for 12 to 24 hours. Repeat the process with a second coat; a third coat may or may not be necessary.

Choose a spray finish that will suit your needs. Use painter's pyramids to prop up your pieces as they dry, and spray on a disposable surface such as the cardboard I'm using here.

Spray varnishes are easy and quick to apply.

For extra protection, you can add a clear heat-resistant spray or brush-on lacquer. You can also use a clear water-resistant spray or brush-on lacquer when using a trivet as a centerpiece on a table with a flowerpot that might get wet, for example. For trivets designed for outdoor use, apply a clear weather-resistant spray or urethane for UV protection. Make sure to allow any final finish to dry completely before you use the piece.

If you are placing a trivet or coaster on a tablecloth or a wooden surface, attaching felt or cork spacers/feet to the bottom is advisable. This will help prevent oil from bleeding into the tablecloth if there is no additional lacquer coating, and it also protects the surface from potential scratches. Felt or cork spacers can be purchased at many hardware, dollar, and craft stores. Make sure that

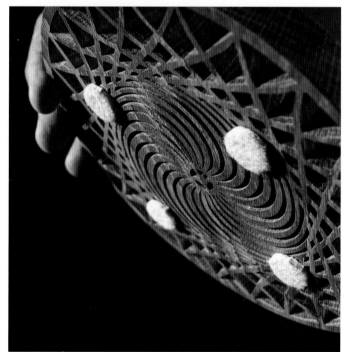

Felt spacers/feet like these add an extra layer of protection to your home's surfaces.

Painting with acrylic paints is an easy way to jazz up a design.

the spacers are thick enough to allow a space between the trivet and tabletop surface.

For coaster finishing, I like to apply a wood sealer first, then two or three coats of a spray varnish or hand-painted varnish such as Varathane® or urethane.

When you plan to use a trivet or plaque for decoration and want to add color, acrylic paints are a good choice. You can buy small jars or plastic bottles from any art supply store. Many dollar-type stores carry them as well. Seal the wood first if you wish, or simply apply the paint directly to the raw wood. After painting is all done, I recommend coating the entire piece with a clear lacquer, such as satin or semi-gloss. If you do not like using spray, use a protective coat of Varathane or urethane. Your local hardware stores will have both, so experiment with finishes to find the ones that work best for you.

PART 2

Gallery of Projects and Ideas

This gallery is meant to get you thinking about possible applications, styles, and finishes you can use when creating the patterns and projects in this book, as well as to give you some contextual examples of projects "in the wild"—how a particular trivet might look on your kitchen counter, how a plaque might look on your garden shed, etc. It will also give you a sneak peek at how different wood choices will affect the final look of a scrolled piece. Flip through and get inspired!

This Peace Coaster, cut from ⅜" (10mm)–thick bamboo, is well protected from hot coffee or tea cups with a spray coating of clear varnish, preferably of a heat-resistant kind.

This Heart Coaster, made from ¼" (6mm)–thick oak, is protected from moisture by spray coating or hand brushing it with a water-resistant varnish such as Varathane or urethane. This coaster has been used for more than ten years with only a couple of coats of spray varnish.

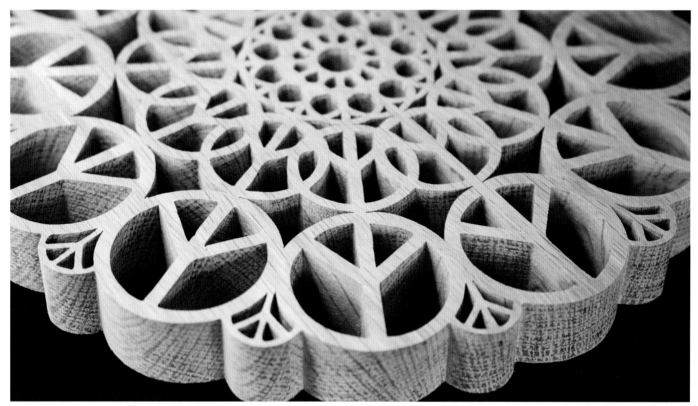

Using thick wood, such as this ¾" (19mm)–thick piece of light-colored oak used for the Peace Trivet, will keep hot plates and pots well away from your countertops, therefore adding an extra layer of protection from heat that may cause damage to surfaces.

As holidays come and go, it is fun to swap out a piece for one that suits the season. Although the Easter Bunny Trivet here was made from ¾" (19mm)–thick oak for use around a stove, it could also be made of many types of woods and thicknesses for everyday use on a table rather than for hot pots. Trivets can be used for virtually anything—a flowerpot base, a table centerpiece, the possibilities are endless.

Experiment with cuts that go part of the way into the outer border of the design, such as the flower petals and wings of the Butterfly Plaque or the tips of the snowflake of the Snowflake Trivet. They can add an interesting touch to a design.

Stack cutting is a great way to make many coasters quickly. Various types of wood, such as bamboo, oak, and maple, make for great stack cuttings and can be cut in two or three layers, depending on the thickness of the wood. For coasters, I like to use wood no thicker than ⅜" (10mm). Pictured here are two Peace Coasters that were stack cut, as well as a Heart Coaster. See instructions for the stack cutting technique on page 22.

This Delicate Spiral Trivet is for use around the kitchen for hot pots. There are products that can be used to heat-treat any trivet, but my preference is to simply apply two or three coats of Danish oil and nothing else. Over time, a trivet may show signs of wear and light burn marks, but it can be sanded and refinished.

I designed the Butterfly Plaque with the intention of hanging it on our garden shed. For this purpose, I cut it out of 1" (25mm)–thick cedar and sprayed it with three coats of clear exterior-grade gloss varnish. If you are making any project for the outdoors, I suggest that you refinish it over time, since it will be affected by weather, UV light, rain, etc. I love how this plaque accents our shed and garden. During the winter months, it hangs inside our house on our living room wall.

A project with thick uncut areas, like the Shamrock Trivet, is good for beginners, but you'll still have to pay attention to the little bridge areas in this particular pattern. The finer the detail, the more risk for breakage, especially if the piece is dropped or bumped.

When cutting lines from a fret like in the fish tail in the Angelfish Bowl Trivet/Plaque, pay special attention to backing the blade out of each line and then into the next. Forcing a blade out through the line may cause breakage to the section you are working on.

The Summer Love Plaque is shown here on exterior window shutters. I made these out of ¼" (6mm)–thick Baltic birch plywood, then applied acrylic paint colors. I spray coated them with three layers of clear exterior-grade gloss varnish. This is a sheltered area, meaning that there is not much of an issue with rain or heavy weather, so the Baltic birch plywood works well, but where there is heavier weather, consider using cedar, pine, or even teak. These woods weather well when painted and coated with exterior-grade varnish.

Many of the patterns in this book can be transformed into other kinds of functional projects, such as a lazy Susan. A simple way to make a lazy Susan (like this one, the Spring Flower Lazy Susan) is to purchase a lazy Susan, disassemble it, and then scroll saw the top piece. See instructions for creating this project on page 48.

One aesthetic choice you can make is to use wood pieces with strong, visible grains like this piece of ¾" (19mm)–thick oak used for the Starflake Trivet. I prefer oak over most other woods, mainly because of the availability in my area, but many hardwoods can be used. I also love the wood grain that is often available when using oak. The grain adds a very nice texture and is visually pleasing.

PART 3

Step-by-Step Projects

This section of the book features three diverse projects presented in a step-by-step format. The first project is a solid introduction to all parts of the project process, not only the scrolling but the prep and finishing as well. The second project is a great example of how to customize pattern borders and add hardware. And the third project gives you a look at how to add a background and paint your designs.

For a printable PDF of the patterns used in this book, please contact Fox Chapel Publishing at customerservice@foxchapelpublishing.com, stating the ISBN and title of the book in the subject line, along with details of the pattern(s) you require.

Note: Pattern fret lines appear in red for contrast with the gray frets of the pattern, and "+" symbols indicate drill holes.

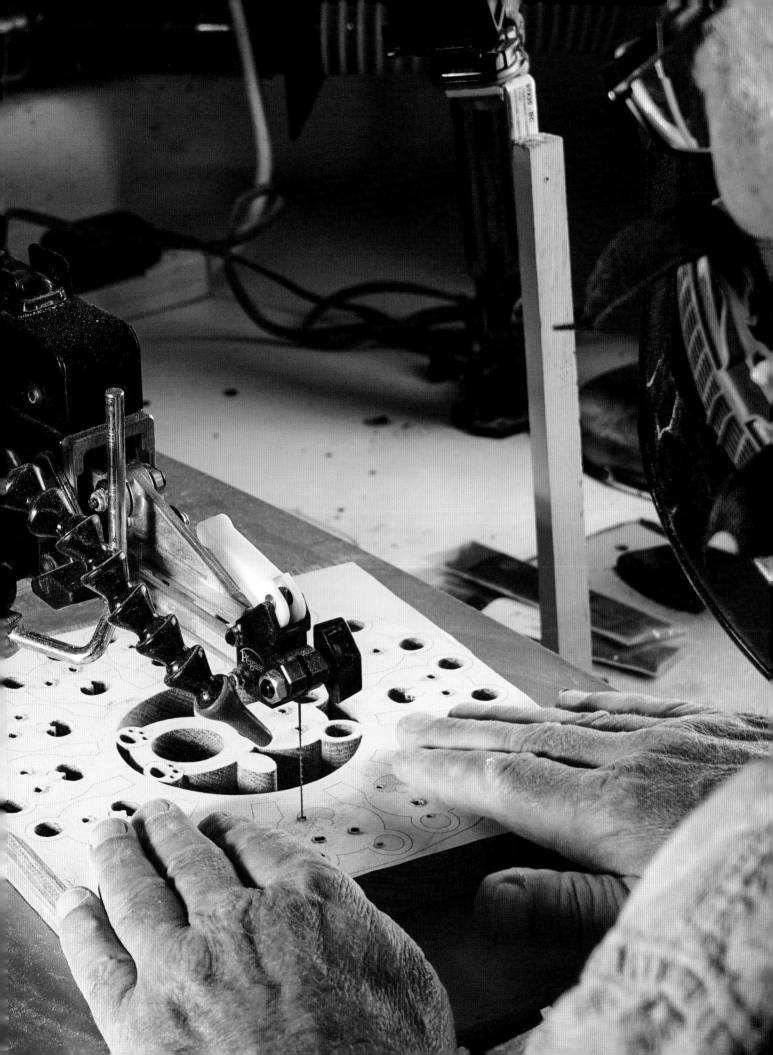

Teddy Bear Trivet

Teddies make a cute gift for a child—or a child at heart! Follow along with this project for a great introduction to all parts of the project process.

Beginner

Actual size

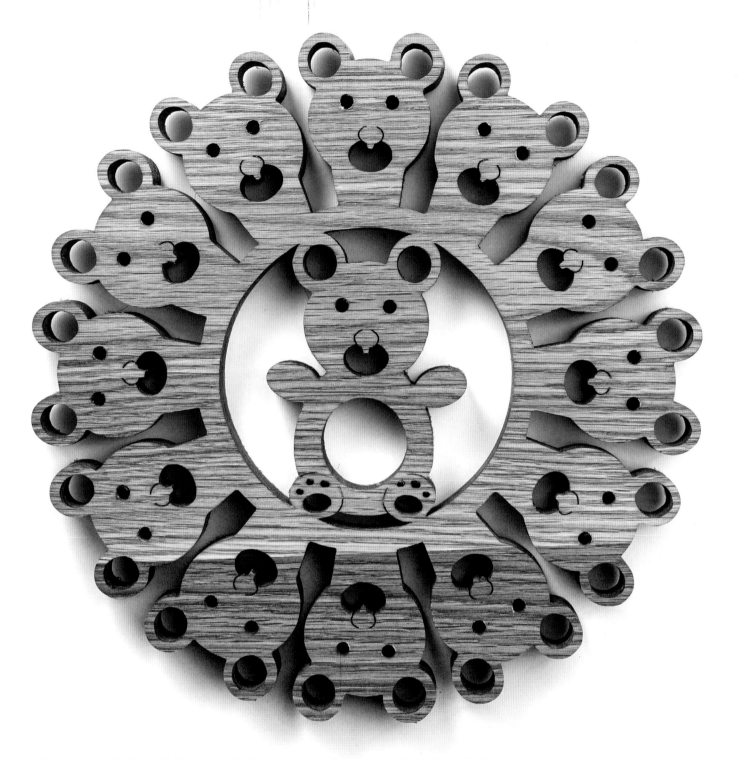

- **Recommended wood:** Hardwood of choice, ½"–¾" (13–19mm) thick, 8½" (21.6cm) square
- **Recommended drill bits:** ¹⁄₁₆" (1.6mm) for interior cutouts. Bear eyes (26 places): ⅛" (3.2mm).
- **Recommended blades:** #5 reverse skip-tooth or reverse tooth
- **Notes/special instructions:** A steady hand will produce great results.
- **Recommended finishing:** Danish oil or oil of choice

1

Measure your square blank approximately ½" (1.3cm) larger than the pattern design.

2

Cut the blank. For this step, a radial arm saw (pictured) or sliding compound saw works well, but you can use any saw.

3

Cut carefully along the outside of the line.

4

Sand the wood blank on both top and bottom. I used a palm sander, but you can also use sandpaper.

5 Clean the wood thoroughly with a tack cloth, removing all dust and ensuring you have a clean, smooth surface prior to attaching the contact paper and pattern in the following steps.

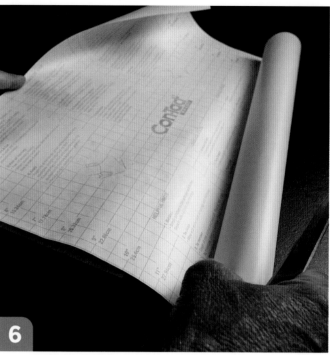

6 Measure and cut a piece of contact paper to the same width as the wood blank, peel the backing off the paper, and apply the sticky side to the wood.

7 Cut out the pattern, apply spray glue to the back side, wait 30 seconds to 1 minute for the glue to become tacky, and then apply the pattern to the contact paper.

8 Drill all the pilot holes, including the bear eyes of the desired diameter. If possible, use a drill bit to match the size of the eyes—the drill bit diameter suggested for the eyes is ⅛" (3.2mm). Then sand the back side of the blank to remove the rough edges created by the drill bit.

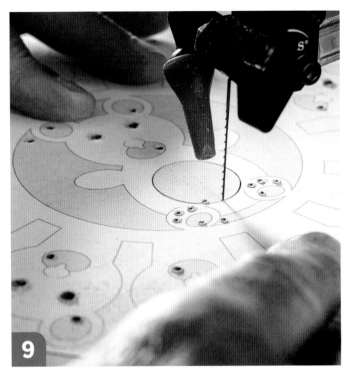

9

Start by scroll sawing the center of the bear's belly.

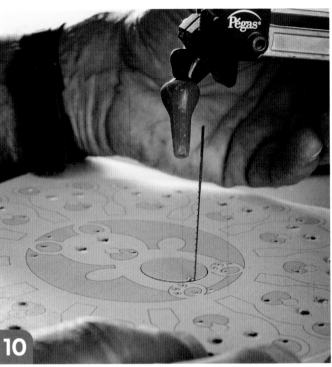

10

When you're done with the bear's belly, remove the blade to move it to a different pilot hole.

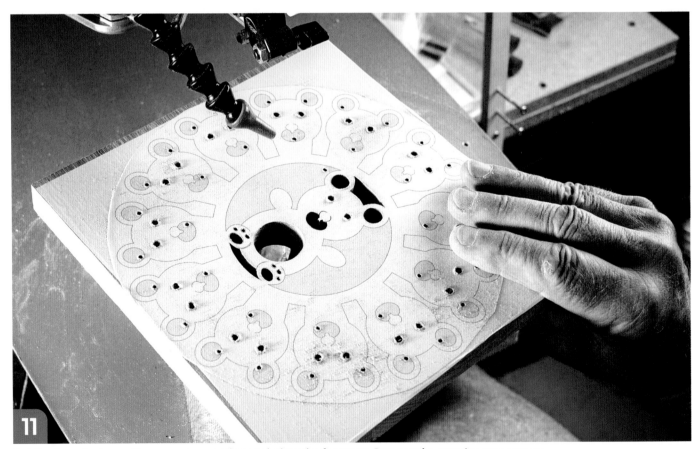

11

Cut the toes, feet, mouth, ear centers, and space below the feet next. Pop out the cut pieces as you go.

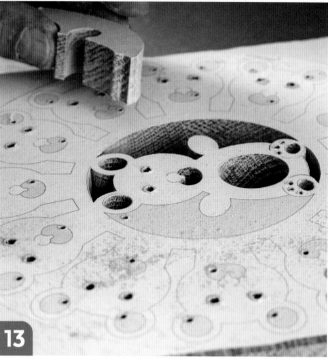

12 Each time you start a new fret, carefully thread the blade up through the pilot hole without overly bending it. Bending the blade too much will cause a kink or potentially weaken it.

13 After finishing the bear's features, scroll saw the space to either side of the bear.

14 Here is the finished central bear. Make sure to periodically brush away excess sawdust so that it doesn't get in your way as you proceed.

15

Next, cut all the mouths and ears of the surrounding bear heads.

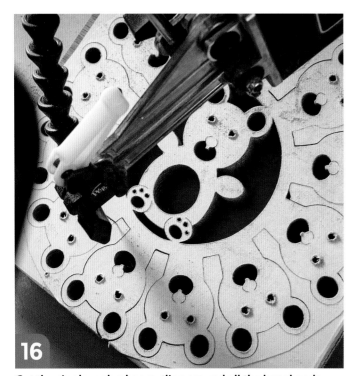

16

Cut the single, unbroken outline around all the bear heads.

17

Remove the blade and start to carefully pop the piece out of the blank.

18 Here is the finished fretted piece before cleanup.

19 Remove the pattern from the piece by simply peeling away the contact paper.

20 Sand the piece (see Basic Process, page 17) and finish as desired (see finishing options beginning on page 23).

Spring Flower Lazy Susan

Intermediate

This bouquet features a mix of large and small blooms. This is a great project to make if you're interested in learning how to customize pattern edges and add hardware.

Actual size for an 8" (20.3cm) lazy Susan or trivet; to make a 15" (38cm) lazy Susan, print at 187% for 15" (38cm) dia.

- **Recommended wood:** Hardwood of choice, ½"–¾" (13–19mm) thick, 8½" (21.6cm) square. If you want to make a larger lazy Susan as featured, see step 9 and use a 15" (38cm) dia. pre-purchased lazy Susan or a 15½" (39.4cm) hardwood of choice to create it from scratch.

- **Recommended drill bits:** ³⁄₆₄" (1.2mm) & ¹⁄₁₆" (1.6mm) or #56 (1.2mm) & #52 (1.6mm) for interior cutouts. Large flower center holes (12 places): ³⁄₁₆" (4.8mm); small flower center holes (8 places): ⅛" (3.2mm); center hole (1 place): ⅜" (9.5mm). If making the 15" (38cm) lazy Susan: large flower center holes (12 places): ¹¹⁄₃₂" (8.7mm); small flower center holes (8 places): ⁷⁄₃₂" (5.5mm); center hole (1 place): ¹¹⁄₁₆" (17.4mm).

- **Recommended blades:** #5 reverse skip-tooth or reverse tooth

- **Notes/special instructions:** Be careful along the border not to accidentally cut into the flower petals.

- **Recommended finishing:** Danish oil or oil of choice

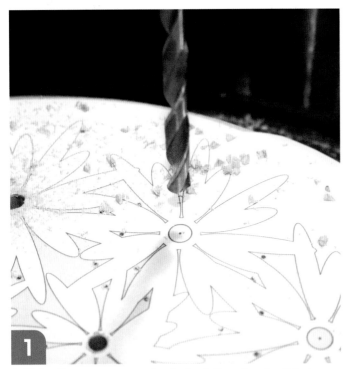

1 Drill the flower centers to the desired diameters (as listed on page 49); this will remove the need to scroll saw them later.

2 Drill all the pilot holes.

3 Start cutting from the middle of the pattern.

4

Continue working your way outward.

5

You can either use the outline provided on the pattern or draw the outline you want with the last flower petals touching/connecting to the rim. When I took these photos, I was using a version of the pattern that didn't have the outline rim on it yet, so I had to manually add it. You can make a similar alteration to any pattern you like.

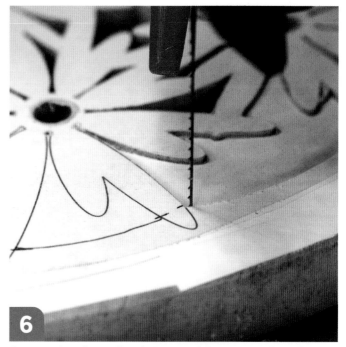

6

Start cutting the outline, being careful not to accidentally cut through the flower petals.

7 Keep cutting all the way around the outline.

8 Once you have finished the last cut, remove the pattern and sand all surfaces.

9

To make this project, I purchased a 15" (38cm)–diameter lazy Susan from IKEA, removed the bearing set from the underside, scrolled the design using the top part, and then reattached the bottom.

10

Make sure you complete all desired finishing steps on the scrolled piece before reattaching the base to the underside of the wood with a polyurethane-based glue or superglue of choice.

11

This design is busy and dense enough that the lazy Susan base isn't very visible from above and doesn't disrupt the look of the design.

Summer Love Plaque

The positivity of summer is really apparent in this welcoming design. Follow along to learn how to add a background and paint your design.

Intermediate

Print at actual size for 8" (20.3cm) dia., at 125% for 10" (25.4cm) dia., or at 150% for 12" (30.5cm) dia.

- **Recommended wood:** Baltic birch, ¼"–½" (6–13mm) thick, or any wood of choice, ½"–¾" (13–19mm) thick, 8¾" (22.2cm), 10¾" (27.3cm), or 12¾" (32.4cm) square. To make the featured background, use a second piece of wood sized up at least 1" (2.5cm) larger than your design blank.

- **Recommended drill bits:** ¹⁄₁₆" (1.6mm)

- **Recommended blades:** #3–#5 reverse tooth for Baltic birch; #3–#5 reverse tooth or skip-tooth for other types of wood

- **Notes/special instructions:** Be careful when cutting the fragile flower stems.

- **Recommended finishing:** For hardwood, Danish oil or oil of choice; for Baltic birch plywood, acrylic paints of choice and clear protective brush-on or spray-coat finish

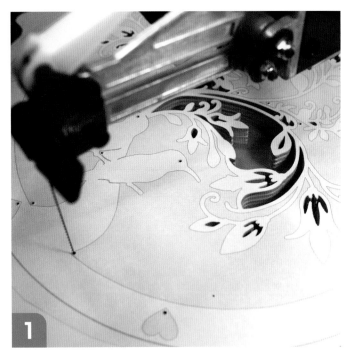

1

Start by drilling all the pilot holes. Also drill the birds' eyes using the same 1/16" (1.6mm) drill bit. First cut the center section above the two birds, then cut all the flower centers within the branches.

2

Next, start cutting the sections that butt up against the outside border.

3

Cut out each section completely before moving onto the next.

4 Cut the outer rim hearts and the outline around the extending bird tail and wing tip.

5 Use a compass to make a large circular pattern in your desired size for the background piece. Apply it to a fresh wood blank like you would a normal pattern, using contact paper, and cut it out. I made mine about ½" (1.3cm) wider than the main design.

6 Thoroughly sand the front and back sides of each piece. Check that you are happy with your mockup before proceeding to the painting steps. I made two for a set of shutters.

7 Paint the first layer of colors. I used basic acrylic craft paint. Allow the first layer of colors to dry and then add finishing touches or additional layers. You can also add more layers while the first layer is still wet and blend.

8

For example, I painted the two center birds completely red, then mixed acrylic colors to get the effect that I wanted for the wings, beak, and head area. I did the same for the plant, flowers, and other birds—I started with solid colors and then added layers of other colors to get the desired effect.

9

Paint the background piece in your desired color; I went with a sky blue here. Attach the scrolled piece to the background using a polyurethane-based glue. If you're going to use the piece outside like I did, spray coat the entire piece with an exterior-grade clear coat to protect it from the elements.

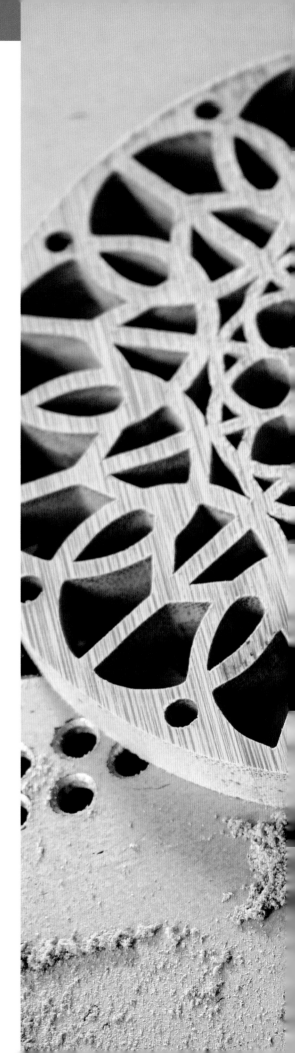

PART 4

Patterns

Here's what you've been waiting for: 24 (more) patterns to choose from and scroll! There are trivets, coasters, and wall plaques aplenty. Suggested uses for each pattern, based on size and complexity, are given in the names of the patterns, but remember: you can use each pattern for whatever you want. Almost every pattern is given at full size for easy photocopying, and each design is accompanied by recommended woods, drill bits, blade sizes and types, and finishing options, so you have everything you need to get scrolling.

For a printable PDF of the patterns used in this book, please contact Fox Chapel Publishing at customerservice@foxchapelpublishing.com, stating the ISBN and title of the book in the subject line, along with details of the pattern(s) you require.

Note: Pattern fret lines appear in red for contrast with the gray frets of the pattern, and "+" symbols indicate drill holes.

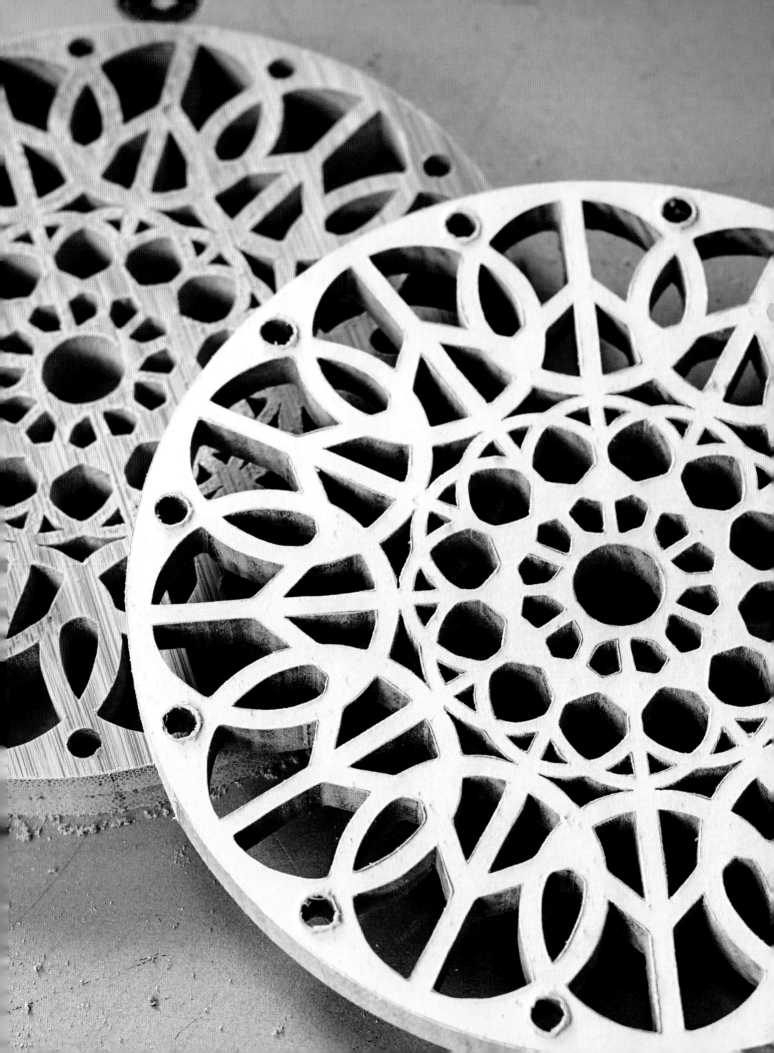

Starflake Trivet

Advanced

Challenge yourself with the many delicate arms of this design.

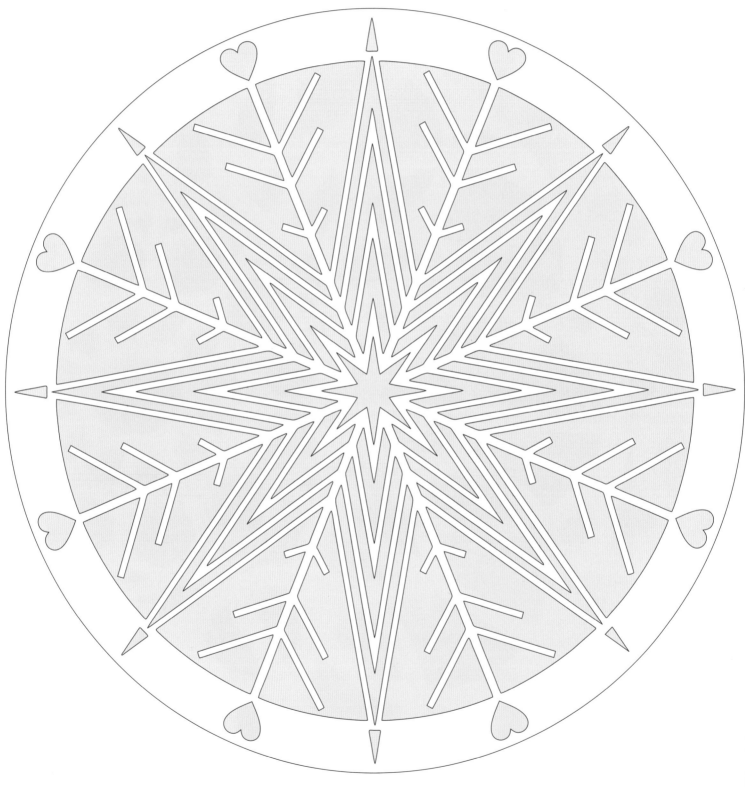

Actual size

- **Recommended wood:** Hardwood of choice, ½"–¾" (13–19mm) thick, 8½" (21.6cm) square
- **Recommended drill bits:** ³⁄₆₄" (1.2mm) & ¹⁄₁₆" (1.6mm) or #56 (1.2mm) & #52 (1.6mm)
- **Recommended blades:** #5 reverse skip-tooth or reverse tooth
- **Notes/special instructions:** Be careful not to waver when cutting the straight lines. A steady hand is needed.
- **Recommended finishing:** Danish oil or oil of choice

Peace Trivet

Intermediate

Get into the groovy vibe of this many-layered design.

Actual size

- **Recommended wood:** Hardwood of choice, ½"–¾" (13–19mm) thick, 8½" (21.6cm) square
- **Recommended drill bits:** ³⁄₆₄" (1.2mm) & ¹⁄₁₆" (1.6mm) or #56 (1.2mm) & #52 (1.6mm)
- **Recommended blades:** #5 reverse skip-tooth or reverse tooth
- **Notes/special instructions:** A steady hand is required when cutting circles.
- **Recommended finishing:** Danish oil or oil of choice

Happy Day Trivet

The interlocking loops of the circles in this design create interesting patterns.

Actual size

- **Recommended wood:** Hardwood of choice, ½"–¾" (13–19mm) thick, 8½" (21.6cm) square

- **Recommended drill bits:** ¾₄" (1.2mm) & ¹⁄₁₆" (1.6mm) or #56 (1.2mm) & #52 (1.6mm) for interior cutouts. Happy face eyes (24 places): ⅛" (3.2mm); center hole (1 place): ¼" (6.4mm).

- **Recommended blades:** #5 reverse skip-tooth or reverse tooth

- **Notes/special instructions:** Take care when cutting circles. Be careful of cutting too quickly.

- **Recommended finishing:** Danish oil or oil of choice

Easter Bunny Trivet

Intermediate

This design is perfect for ringing in the spring season.

Actual size

- **Recommended wood:** Hardwood of choice, ½"–¾" (13–19mm) thick, 8½" (21.6cm) square

- **Recommended drill bits:** ³⁄₆₄" (1.2mm) & ¹⁄₁₆" (1.6mm) or #56 (1.2mm) & #52 (1.6mm) for interior cutouts. Large egg center holes (32 places): ³⁄₃₂" (2.4mm); small egg center holes (72 places): ³⁄₆₄" (1.2mm) or #56 (1.2mm); center hole (1 place): ¼" (6.4mm).

- **Recommended blades:** #5 reverse skip-tooth or reverse tooth

- **Notes/special instructions:** Be careful when drilling the small egg holes. For precise hole locations, a very steady hand is needed.

- **Recommended finishing:** Danish oil or oil of choice

Shamrock Trivet

Beginner/Intermediate

You'll feel lucky when you're working on this delightful design.

Actual size

- ■ **Recommended wood:** Hardwood of choice, ½"–¾" (13–19mm) thick, 8½" (21.6cm) square
- ■ **Recommended drill bits:** ¹⁄₁₆" (1.6mm)
- ■ **Recommended blades:** #5 reverse skip-tooth or reverse tooth
- ■ **Notes/special instructions:** Take your time; a steady hand is needed here for precise cutting.
- ■ **Recommended finishing:** Danish oil or oil of choice

Delicate Spiral Trivet

Intermediate/Advanced

This eye-catching design is a challenge, but it's well worth the effort.

Actual size

- **Recommended wood:** Hardwood of choice, ½"–¾" (13–19mm) thick, 8½" (21.6cm) square

- **Recommended drill bits:** ³⁄₆₄" (1.2mm) & ¹⁄₁₆" (1.6mm) or #56 (1.2mm) & #52 (1.6mm)

- **Recommended blades:** #5 reverse skip-tooth or reverse tooth

- **Notes/special instructions:** Special attention is needed so as not to waver when cutting the spiral lines. Use a steady hand, or the spiral will not be uniform.

- **Recommended finishing:** Danish oil or oil of choice

Snowflake Trivet

Intermediate

Enjoy the chilly points and angles of this snowflake look.

Actual size

- **Recommended wood:** Hardwood of choice, ½"–¾" (13–19mm) thick, 8½" (21.6cm) square

- **Recommended drill bits:** ¹⁄₁₆" (1.6mm) for interior cutouts. Rim holes (16 places): ³⁄₁₆" (4.8mm).

- **Recommended blades:** #5 reverse skip-tooth or reverse tooth

- **Notes/special instructions:** Be careful, as a steady hand is needed for cutting the straight lines of the star shape.

- **Recommended finishing:** Danish oil or oil of choice

Angelfish Bowl Trivet/Plaque

Intermediate

Bring a school of
wooden fish to life!

Actual size

- **Recommended wood:** Baltic birch, ¼"–½" (6–13mm) thick, or hardwood of choice, ½"–¾" (13–19mm) thick, 8½" x 10" (21.6 x 25.4cm) rectangle

- **Recommended drill bits:** ¹⁄₁₆" (1.6mm) for interior cutouts. Fish eye holes (10 places): ³⁄₃₂" (2.4mm).

- **Recommended blades:** #3 reverse tooth for Baltic birch; #5 reverse skip-tooth or reverse tooth for hardwood

- **Notes/special instructions:** Be careful, as a steady hand is needed for cutting the exterior bowl shape.

- **Recommended finishing:** For hardwood, Danish oil or oil of choice; for Baltic birch plywood, acrylic paints of choice and clear protective brush-on or spray-coat finish

Hummingbird Trivet/Plaque

Intermediate/Advanced

This design is as delicate as the birds it depicts.

Print at actual size for 8" (20.3cm) dia. or at 125% for 10" (25.4cm) dia.

- **Recommended wood:** Baltic birch, ¼"–½" (6–13mm) thick, or hardwood of choice, ½"–¾" (13–19mm) thick, 8½" (21.6cm) or 10½" (26.7cm) square when increasing actual size of pattern to 125% for 10" (25.4cm) dia.

- **Recommended drill bits:** ³⁄₆₄" (1.2mm) & ¹⁄₁₆" (1.6mm) or #56 (1.2mm) & #52 (1.6mm) for interior cutouts. Center hole (1 place): ⅜" (9.5mm).

- **Recommended blades:** #3–#5 reverse tooth for Baltic birch; #5 reverse skip-tooth or reverse tooth for hardwood

- **Notes/special instructions:** Be careful to keep your cuts uniform when cutting the hummingbird tails.

- **Recommended finishing:** For hardwood, Danish oil or oil of choice; for Baltic birch plywood, acrylic paints of choice and clear protective brush-on or spray-coat finish

Butterfly Plaque

This standout butterfly is a joy to scroll.

Print at actual size for 8" (20.3cm) dia. or at 125% for 10" (25.4cm) dia.

- **Recommended wood:** Baltic birch, ¼"–½" (6–13mm) thick, or any wood of choice, ½"–¾" (13–19mm) thick, 8½" (21.6cm) or 10½" (26.7cm) square when increasing actual size of pattern to 125% for 10" (25.4cm) dia.

- **Recommended drill bits:** ³⁄₆₄" (1.2mm) & ¹⁄₁₆" (1.6mm) or #56 (1.2mm) & #52 (1.6mm) for interior cutouts. Flower center holes (6 places): ⅜" (9.5mm).

- **Recommended blades:** #3–#5 reverse tooth for Baltic birch; #5 reverse skip-tooth or reverse tooth for hardwood; alternatively, use #0–#1 spiral

- **Notes/special instructions:** Pay special attention when cutting the butterfly antennae, as this is a fragile area to cut.

- **Recommended finishing:** For most woods, Danish oil or oil of choice; for Baltic birch plywood, acrylic paints of choice and clear protective brush-on or spray-coat finish. For exterior use, spar urethane or exterior-grade clear-coat spray.

Ornate Flower Trivet

Intermediate

This design features a great combination of smooth curves and sharp angles.

Actual size

- **Recommended wood:** Hardwood of choice, ½"–¾" (13–19mm) thick, 8½" (21.6cm) square
- **Recommended drill bits:** ¹⁄₁₆" (1.6mm)
- **Recommended blades:** #5 reverse skip-tooth or reverse tooth
- **Notes/special instructions:** Only an even and steady hand is needed for all interior cuts.
- **Recommended finishing:** Danish oil or oil of choice

Sunburst Trivet/Plaque

Intermediate

This prickly design is tricky, but it's easier than it looks!

Actual size

- **Recommended wood:** Baltic birch, ¼"–½" (6–13mm) thick, or any wood of choice, ½"–¾" (13–19mm) thick, 8½" (21.6cm) or 10½" (26.7cm) square when increasing actual size of pattern to 125% for 10" (25.4cm) dia.

- **Recommended drill bits:** ³⁄₆₄" (1.2mm) & ¹⁄₁₆" (1.6mm) or #56 (1.2mm) & #52 (1.6mm) for interior cutouts. Center hole (1 place): ¼" (6.4mm).

- **Recommended blades:** #3–#5 reverse tooth for Baltic birch; #5 reverse skip-tooth or reverse tooth for hardwood

- **Notes/special instructions:** Pay special attention when cutting all straight lines; a steady hand is needed to produce an even flow.

- **Recommended finishing:** For most woods, Danish oil or oil of choice; for Baltic birch plywood, acrylic paints of choice and clear protective brush-on or spray-coat finish. For exterior use, spar urethane or exterior-grade clear-coat spray.

Seahorse Trivet

Advanced

Take your time executing this extremely intricate design.

Print at 125% for 10" (25.4cm) dia.

- **Recommended wood:** Baltic birch, ¼"–½" (6–13mm) thick, or any wood of choice, ½"–¾" (13–19mm) thick, 10½" (26.7cm) square when increasing actual size of pattern to 125% for 10" (25.4cm) dia.

- **Recommended drill bits:** ³⁄₆₄" (1.2mm) & ¹⁄₁₆" (1.6mm) or #56 (1.2mm) & #52 (1.6mm)

- **Recommended blades:** #3–#5 reverse tooth for Baltic birch; #5 reverse skip-tooth or reverse tooth for hardwood

- **Notes/special instructions:** This piece has many cutouts, so patience and a steady hand are essential.

- **Recommended finishing:** For hardwood, Danish oil or oil of choice; for Baltic birch plywood, acrylic paints of choice and clear protective brush-on or spray-coat finish

Guitar Trivet

Beginner/Intermediate

This piece is perfect for the music lover in your life.

Actual size

- **Recommended wood:** Hardwood of choice, ½"–¾" (13–19mm) thick, 8½" (21.6cm) square
- **Recommended drill bits:** ¹⁄₁₆" (1.6mm)
- **Recommended blades:** #5 reverse skip-tooth or reverse tooth
- **Notes/special instructions:** Take your time; only a steady hand is needed here for precise cutting.
- **Recommended finishing:** Danish oil or oil of choice

Mandala Trivet

Intermediate

The classic shape of this mandala will calm you as you work.

Actual size

- ■ **Recommended wood:** Hardwood of choice, ½"–¾" (13–19mm) thick, 8½" (21.6cm) square

- ■ **Recommended drill bits:** ³⁄₆₄" (1.2mm) & ¹⁄₁₆" (1.6mm) or #56 (1.2mm) & #52 (1.6mm) for interior cutouts. Center hole (1 place): ¼" (6.4mm).

- ■ **Recommended blades:** #5 reverse skip-tooth or reverse tooth

- ■ **Notes/special instructions:** Be careful when cutting the center section. This area requires a steady hand and precise cuts.

- ■ **Recommended finishing:** Danish oil or oil of choice

Fancy Circle Trivet

Intermediate

The triangles in this design help to draw the eye outward.

Actual size

- **Recommended wood:** Hardwood of choice, ½"–¾" (13–19mm) thick, 8½" (21.6cm) square
- **Recommended drill bits:** 1⁄16" (1.6mm) for interior cutouts. Triangle holes (12 places): ¼" (6.4mm).
- **Recommended blades:** #5 reverse skip-tooth or reverse tooth
- **Notes/special instructions:** A slow and easy approach will produce quality work.
- **Recommended finishing:** Danish oil or oil of choice

Square Spiral Trivet

Intermediate

The squares and spiral form a nice contrast.

Actual size

- **Recommended wood:** Hardwood of choice, ½"–¾" (13–19mm) thick, 8½" (21.6cm) square

- **Recommended drill bits:** ¾₄" (1.2mm) & ⅙₆" (1.6mm) or #56 (1.2mm) & #52 (1.6mm) for interior cutouts. Holes on outside of spiral (24 places): ⅙₆" (1.6mm).

- **Recommended blades:** #5 reverse skip-tooth or reverse tooth

- **Notes/special instructions:** Special attention is needed when cutting the spiral lines, or the spiral will not be uniform.

- **Recommended finishing:** Danish oil or oil of choice

Christmas Tree Trivet

Beginner

Ring in the winter season with this arboreal design.

Actual size

- **Recommended wood:** Hardwood or any wood of choice, ½"–¾" (13–19mm) thick, 8½" (21.6cm) square

- **Recommended drill bits:** ⅟₁₆" (1.6mm) for interior cutouts. Tree and perimeter holes (40 places): ³⁄₁₆" (4.8mm); center hole (1 place): ½" (13mm).

- **Recommended blades:** #5 reverse skip-tooth or reverse tooth

- **Notes/special instructions:** A steady hand will produce great results.

- **Recommended finishing:** For hardwood, Danish oil or oil of choice. Alternatively, you can use acrylic paint if not planning to use the trivet near a hot stove. If using paint, I recommend adding a clear-coat spray or hand-applied clear coat.

Heart Coaster

Intermediate

Let the hearts here speak volumes to the piece's recipient.

Actual size for standard coaster;
for other uses, print at 160% for 8" (20.3cm) dia.
or at 200% for 10" (25.4cm) dia.

- **Recommended wood:** Any wood of choice, ¼"–⅜" (6–10mm) thick, 5½" (14cm) square
- **Recommended drill bits:** ¹⁄₁₆" (1.6mm) for interior cutouts. Perimeter holes above hearts (8 places): ¹¹⁄₆₄" (4.4mm); center hole (1 place): ⅜" (9.5mm).
- **Recommended blades:** #3–#5 reverse skip-tooth or reverse tooth
- **Notes/special instructions:** A steady hand will produce great results.
- **Recommended finishing:** Danish oil or oil of choice, and/or clear protective brush-on or spray-coat finish to help protect wood surface from moisture

Peace Coaster

Intermediate

This is a simple but solid design with a lovely message of peace.

Actual size for standard coaster;
for other uses, print at 160% for 8" (20.3cm) dia.
or at 200% for 10" (25.4cm) dia.

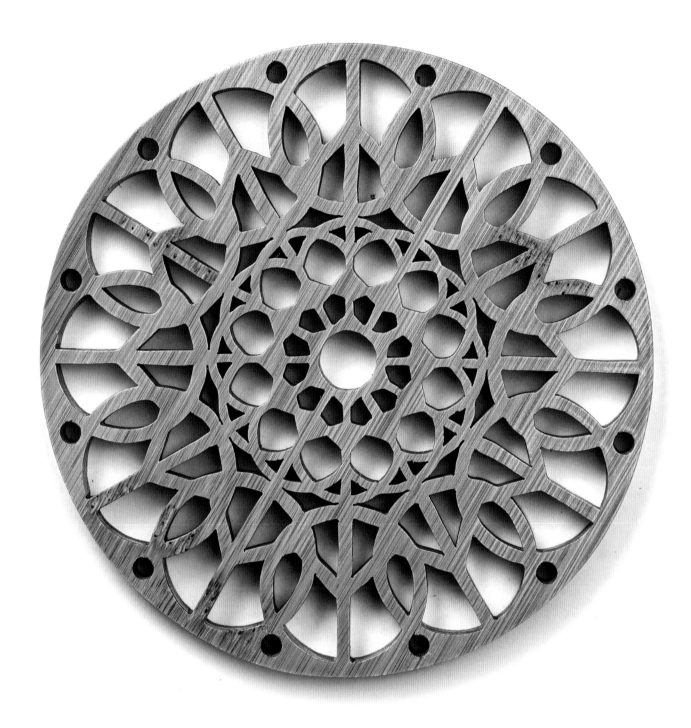

- **Recommended wood:** Any wood of choice, ¼"–⅜" (6–10mm) thick, 5½" (14cm) square

- **Recommended drill bits:** ¹⁄₁₆" (1.6mm) for interior cutouts. Perimeter holes (12 places): ³⁄₁₆" (4.8mm).

- **Recommended blades:** #3–#5 reverse skip-tooth or reverse tooth

- **Notes/special instructions:** A steady hand when cutting circles will produce great results.

- **Recommended finishing:** Danish oil or oil of choice, and/or clear protective brush-on or spray-coat finish to help protect wood surface from moisture

Anchor Coaster

Beginner/Intermediate

Set out to sea with this design!

Actual size for standard coaster;
for other uses, print at 160% for 8" (20.3cm) dia.
or at 200% for 10" (25.4cm) dia.

- **Recommended wood:** Any wood of choice, ¼"–⅜" (6–10mm) thick, 5½" (14cm) square
- **Recommended drill bits:** ¹⁄₁₆" (1.6mm) for interior cutouts. Anchor link holes (8 places): ⅛" (3.2mm).
- **Recommended blades:** #3–#5 reverse skip-tooth or reverse tooth
- **Notes/special instructions:** Be careful when cutting the center section. Keep steady when cutting those thin lines.
- **Recommended finishing:** Danish oil or oil of choice, and/or clear protective brush-on or spray-coat finish to help protect wood surface from moisture

Elaborate Plaque

Intermediate

This design
really draws
the eye in.

Actual size

- **Recommended wood:** Baltic birch, ¼"–½" (6–13mm) thick, or any wood of choice, ½"–¾" (13–19mm) thick, 8" x 10½" (20.3 x 26.7cm) rectangle

- **Recommended drill bits:** ³⁄₆₄" (1.2mm) & ¹⁄₁₆" (1.6mm) or #56 (1.2mm) & #52 (1.6mm)

- **Recommended blades:** #3–#5 reverse tooth for Baltic birch; #5 reverse skip-tooth or reverse tooth for other types of wood

- **Notes/special instructions:** Pay special attention when cutting the center section, as a steady hand is needed here to produce even lines.

- **Recommended finishing:** For most woods, Danish oil or oil of choice; for Baltic birch plywood, acrylic paints of choice and clear protective brush-on or spray-coat finish

Dragonfly Plaque

Use a hardwood with a dramatic grain
to help this insect take flight.

Print at 133% for 10" (25.4cm) dia.

- **Recommended wood:** Baltic birch, ¼"–½" (6–13mm) thick, or any wood of choice, ½"–¾" (13–19mm) thick, 11" (27.9cm) square

- **Recommended drill bits:** ³⁄₆₄" (1.2mm) & ¹⁄₁₆" (1.6mm) or #56 (1.2mm) & #52 (1.6mm) for interior cutouts. Flower center holes (8 places): ⁷⁄₁₆" (11.1mm).

- **Recommended blades:** #3–#5 reverse tooth for Baltic birch; #3–#5 reverse skip-tooth or reverse tooth for other types of wood; alternatively, use #0–#1 spiral to cut the interior section of the dragonfly

- **Notes/special instructions:** Be careful when cutting the left rear leg, as this will be fragile if cut too soon.

- **Recommended finishing:** For hardwood, Danish oil or oil of choice; for Baltic birch plywood, acrylic paints of choice and clear protective brush-on or spray-coat finish

Spring Flower Plaque

Intermediate

A burst of blooms will bring joy to anyone.

Print at 133% for 10" (25.4cm) dia.

- **Recommended wood:** Baltic birch, ¼"–½" (6–13mm) thick, or any wood of choice, ½"–¾" (13–19mm) thick, 10½" (26.7cm) square

- **Recommended drill bits:** ³⁄₆₄" (1.2mm) & ¹⁄₁₆" (1.6mm) or #56 (1.2mm) & #52 (1.6mm) for interior cutouts. Large flower holes (12 places): ¼" (6.4mm); small flower holes (8 places): ¹¹⁄₆₄" (4.4mm); center hole (1 place): ½" (12.7mm).

- **Recommended blades:** #3–#5 reverse tooth for Baltic birch; #3–#5 reverse skip-tooth or reverse tooth for other types of wood over ½" (13mm) thick

- **Notes/special instructions:** Be careful when cutting the center section. A steady hand is needed to cut a smooth circle.

- **Recommended finishing:** For hardwood, Danish oil or oil of choice; for Baltic birch plywood, acrylic paints of choice and clear protective brush-on or spray-coat finish

About the Author

Born in 1951 in Westmount, Quebec, Canada, Charles R. Hand grew up in a small rural town west of Montreal, Quebec. After a successful career in electrical, mechanical, and graphic design and a move to Ontario, Charles started to scroll saw in 2005 as a hobby during the long winter months. He also started to design his own patterns and purchased every scroll saw magazine and book that he could get his hands on. Over the years, his designs became more and more involved as he studied the works of other designers and artists and eventually developed his own style.

Nowadays, one of the first things Charles does when he gets up every morning is turn on his computer to see what he can design for scroll sawing. Many of his designs take 15 to 30 hours to complete. His camera goes wherever he does on the chance that he might see something he wants to turn into a design. He has won several awards for his work in local woodworking and craft shows, but Charles scroll saws mainly because it is rewarding, relaxing, and a great winter hobby. He has drawers full of scrolled portraits and many hanging throughout his house. After writing this book, he now has a house full of trivets and other items that he likes to scroll saw, too. You can find Charles' award-winning work in the pages of *Scroll Saw Woodworking & Crafts* magazine and on his website, *www.scrollsawart4u.weebly.com*.

Acknowledgments

Thank you to my daughter, Carrie, for loving tropical fish, especially angelfish. Thank you to my son, Terry, for choosing photography as a career. Without his help, it would have been a rough go for me to produce the photos needed for this book. Thank you to my stepdaughter, Stephanie, for her love of bears, as she knows which piece was designed for her. Thank you to my stepson, Chris, for also being a fan of my work. I love seeing the look on their faces at Christmas when opening up gifts from me. "Oh . . . (hesitation) . . . thanks . . ." "Oh . . . (hesitation) . . . did you make this?" Always puts a smile on my face to see sheer excitement when they open up their gifts to see yet another scroll saw piece from me. And my grandkids, Larsen and Freya, for saying, "Cool, Grandpa . . . nice."

Thank you to my good friend, Mike Williams, as he has been a solid supporter of my work. If it were not for his friendship and his amazing design work in scroll saw, I may not be where I am today.

Thank you to Fox Chapel's Kerry Bogert for her help with getting this book afloat and Kaylee Schofield for persuading me to write this book, and a special thank you to Colleen Dorsey, who is one awesome writer/editor and a delight to work with. If it were not for her help, there is no way that I would have been able to write this on my own. I also want to thank all the other employees at Fox Chapel for their input.